GOD'S
GIFT
(WOMAN)

Freddie Floyd Jr

ISBN 978-1-63885-001-4 (Paperback)
ISBN 978-1-63885-002-1 (Digital)

Covenant Books, Inc.
11661 Hwy 707
Murrells Inlet, SC 29576
www.covenantbooks.com

To my beautiful daughter, Rayna Elizabeth Floyd. To love thyself is to know thyself. When God blessed me with you, it was one of the proudest moments in my life; you made my light brighter than I ever thought possible. As you continue to grow to adulthood, always remember who you are, and you can do all things that you have passion for in Christ which provides you with all things.

A man serves and leads his family.

Serve and lead may seem like a contradiction, but they are inseparable according to Scripture. While the Apostle Paul tells us in Ephesians 5:23 that "the husband is the head of the wife," he quickly puts to rest any notions that this leadership allows for selfish male dominance. He completes the sentence with, "as Christ also is the head of the church." The passage goes on to say that "husbands should love their wives just as Christ also loved the church and gave Himself up for her" (Ephesians 5:25 KJV). This paints a picture of leadership contrary to how the world views it.

A man is called to be a servant-leader—to take responsibility for his wife and children and to put their needs ahead of his own. He is called to demonstrate selfless, sacrificial love—the type of love we see in God toward his children.

CONTENTS

PREFACE

This book is about the empowerment of women in today's world, including young girls and adult women alike. No two women are the same, nor is every situation; however, what remains the same is God's Word and his commandment of how men should place a high value on the woman. Scripture is noticeably clear when it speaks to love a woman, to honor a woman. My vision is to take you back to God's Word and show you why you must have self-worth, know your value, be respected, and motivate you to get your groove back. You will never change what you tolerate. You can no longer settle for just a man.

ACKNOWLEDGMENTS

The Lord has graciously surrounded me with angels without whom this project would have been impossible. The order in which these angels were listed in no way reflects their importance. I have some strong women in my family that I hold in high regard. Cathy Floyd is at the top of this list. She is my birth mother, and her guidance in my youth has been invaluable. I always say, "There is no greater love than a mother's love."

Betty Stanley (Aunt). She is the closest thing to having two moms; I remember the countless hours of talking to her about any- and everything. She is a particular type of woman.

Mattie Barnes (Aunt). This woman right here has shown me how to look at things differently than others. We have had our share of talks. She made me realize that you cannot control what others do when you decide to allow someone to borrow money. That one saying has helped me out more than you can imagine.

Linda Floyd; Jackie Grier; Janice Bishop; Lottie Floyd; Annie Ruth Floyd; and lastly, but certainly not least, I want to give a special thanks to the oldest of all the angels, my eighty-eight-year-old grandma Janie Ma Hall—all these angels have played significant roles in my life in one way or another.

I thank God for my family. The support they have always given has been instrumental in my success thus far. So, ladies, please take a bow. You deserve it.

INTRODUCTION

Jesus Christ is God made flesh. As such, he embodies all of God's opinions. In his earthly life, Jesus was the visible expression of God himself. By his actions and his words, we discover God's view of a woman. And that view was utterly contrary to the prevailing view of his day and even today.

The life of God was first placed in the womb of a woman before it got to you and to me. And God was pleased.

In Jesus Christ, we find God's view of a woman. Not man's view. Not the American view. Not the European view. Not the Asian view. Not the African view. But God's view.

Consider this. When God decided to make his entrance upon this earth, he visited a woman. He chose a woman to bring forth the Eternal Son, the Messiah—the Anointed One for whom Israel had waited thousands of years for.

Sisters in Christ, this is your Lord's view of a woman. Take your high place. But that is not all. Your Lord allowed an unclean woman to touch the hem of his garment, and he was not ashamed. In fact, he praised her for it. It was the highest compliment he ever gave anyone. He also healed her daughter, and he was not ashamed. This is God's view of a woman.

CHAPTER 1

In the Beginning

Nevertheless, neither is the man without the woman,
neither the woman without the man, in the Lord.
—1 Corinthians 11:11

When you think of the word *woman.*, what is the first thing that comes to your mind? Depending on your experience or encounters you have had, there will be multiple different answers. With the way the people in the world are today, I am sure your concept of a woman is distorted. We live in a time wherein, in my opinion, the word *woman* has been diluted, watered down. Most men, when they think of woman, they believe sex or maybe even control.

Suppose you took time-out to study our history of women in our country or the world for that matter. In almost all cases, *women* have been excluded and, when mentioned, are typically portrayed in sex-stereotypical roles such as wives, mothers, daughters, and mistresses. So how can we think of the woman or see women in a different light? What is a woman's worth?

If you read my first book, you are designed to be successful; you will understand when I say there is a massive difference in how a woman is viewed in this world by men and how Christ viewed women. Well, sometimes in life, you must go back and renew your mind to understand the importance of that word, *woman*, utterly.

Over centuries, women have been devalued time and time again, even by some women, yet we must always seek answers to life by using God's Word in everything. So let us find out how Jesus himself valued women. I mean, that is who we are supposed to follow.

Scripture says speaking of Jesus, "I am the way, the truth, and the Life," so let us dive into it. What does the Word of God say about a woman? In the beginning, God said, "Let us make man in our own image. In the image of God, He created him…" Most people stop right there. Society will pump their chest out and roar, as if to say, "This is a man's world" kind of roar. But it is a funny thing about God. Unlike man, he will finish the work that he started.

God continues and says, "…He created him, male and female." That is a big statement. So unlike the many ways you may have come to understand, God created the male and the female simultaneously, which means you are equally as important to God's plan and will as any creature on earth.

God didn't make a man, give him orders, and exclude the woman. No, He spoke to us in unison. Does Scripture not show you this? You were born spiritually at the same time as a man, which makes us equal in the sight of God. Let that sink in for a moment. Let it sink some more. To top it off, guess what? When God blessed man, he blessed you also.

You see, therefore, it is so important to learn how to read and study the Word on your own. An old Russian proverb says, "*Doveryai, no proveryai,*" which means, "Trust, but verify." Therefore, reading for yourself is so vital in ascertaining what truth is.

It would be best if you continuously verified which, by the way, will make some people a bit upset; however, at least you are not being misled. You see, ladies, you have to shake off how the world has treated you and understand that God has demonstrated the same trust in you as in man. If not, he would not have spoken to you and gave special instruction to you as he did the man. God told them, "'Be fruitful and multiply, and fill the earth, and subdue it, and rule."

So you are a big deal in God's creation and have a right to stand beside the man in this world and rule. Ruling does not mean being placed in a box as if you can only do specific jobs. Once you understand this, there will no need for competition.

Now I know some people will fight against this notion. I am sure it is to be expected. However, I want to stick with Scripture on this matter and leave out feelings and emotions based on gender bias or man's tradition. I like the term most people say to "keep it 100," and my "100" is the Bible. God spoke to us simultaneously and told us, together, to be fruitful and multiply. To multiply, and if my logic is correct, that takes both a male and a female to do that; so it appears there is no us without you.

I am going to go deeper because some of you have been deceived, ladies. So I want to drive this point in like a nail because I do not want you to miss how important a woman is in God's eyes. There has always been this masculine message about the Scripture regarding who was created first in the physical. Okay, I get it. It is hard to argue with facts, and I am sure you have heard this as well. It is like blah, blah, blah. We know man, in the physical sense, God created first, but it is time we stop picking and choosing and teach the whole Bible. Now can I get a little amen from somebody?

While this is true, you cannot pick and choose what God's instruction was and still is for us in this world. While being formed first, God also gave men a particular responsibility, and there was an expectation that God spoke in the Old Testament and the New Testament. He told the formed first man to work. Do you recall that scripture? In essence, God said to man, "I am putting you in this garden. Now work it." God used the word *to dress it*, which ultimately means "to work." To work is the first thing in understanding the importance of a woman to a man; he needs to work. Now God told man before there was any other person to our knowledge around in the garden (Genesis 2:15).

Now, ladies, I want to say—before I go any further—if you see a man that tickles your fancy, you must understand that if he wants to be in your life, he needs to understand he needs to have a job or get a job, and that is that. Remember that is what God told a man to do: to work. And if he is not working, he may not be ready to be the drink of water you so desire.

More importantly, you need to understand he needs to work. Furthermore, ladies, if God told a man to work, the question is now, Why do you house a man that is going against God's order? And, making matters worse, you dare to complain to God about him not being a man. Understanding is a small example of what was meant in Scripture when it says, "My people perish for lack of knowledge" (Hosea 4:6).

We cannot omit what God instructs us to do, and there is no wonder why there is such a lack of understanding of the importance of a woman or even her value. When a man does not want to work, ladies, that is out of God's order. The Bible calls it being idle. Healthy men who are not working should have no purpose in dating anyone until they get it together because you cannot expect him to lead you if he cannot lead himself, and working is God's command to a male. The problem that I have with some women—my issue with some women that I run into is, you will take a broke, nonworking man in and house him, yet complain about a man who is working because he doesn't make enough.

You see, ladies, some of you have it backward. A job is a job. And it does not matter what type of job it is. If it is legal, we have no right to look down on any man just because you may earn more money than he does, because in reality, ladies, as quiet as it's kept if a man is working, he is following God's word.

Now it does not mean he cannot work on improving himself, but he must work. That is the first thing that should attract you to him. He goes to work. He has a job. That is the first thing God told man. So again, being formed first comes with a command to make a living for yourself. If any of us want to get right with God, we must stop choosing what part of the Bible we want to follow. You cannot, as a man, so-called rule over [woman] if you are not willing to do the most straightforward task: to go to work.

Just as a disclaimer, when God told the man to rule over woman, let's understand what that means in its proper context. First he spoke to a woman being a wife and not any random woman; so, boyfriends, stick a sock in it when you expect a girlfriend to submit to you—not happening. Secondly, *rule* means "being responsible for your family"—the good, the bad, and the ugly. Your spouse is not some slave that you say fetch to; she is your life partner, and we must treat her as such.

It is the man's responsibility to make things right when things are wrong, so please allow that to sink in as well. If a man is not ready to be responsible, he is not prepared to be your husband now. Let that sink in, ladies. Men, you are tasked to be an overseer of your family. You are the head, and this does not mean ownership.

Why do you suppose God instructed husbands to love their wives as their bodies? It is because he who loves his wife loves himself. And there is no man alive—at least, in his right mind—who wants to hurt himself. So, ladies, I hope this gives you a better understanding of how important you are so I may continue.

In the spiritual form, he told them both to rule the Earth, so let us get that clear. God gave the ability to lead or oversee in this life to both male and female, but here is where God truly sets the woman apart from the man—besides the natural brute strength—which so many people seem to not understand, or they do not care. This is particularly important to any man that wants to love a woman and to one day marry her.

When God decided to make someone suitable for the man, Scripture says everything needed for her comfort was already created. *Boom*, and there it is. Men, read that part again. Now, ladies, you read that part again. I understand we should work together, but before we disobeyed God, that is the way it went down. He did not tell her to go to work, as he said to the man. This is a huge deal when understanding who you are in the sight of God; therefore, I say a woman is a gift from God. You were supposed to be taken care of, period. It is like God is saying, "Man, go to work, and when you have worked, I will bring something pleasant to the eye. But you must take tender care of what I am about to give you."

Now, ladies, disclaimer alert. Always remember you are to be his helper, his partner, so there may be times where you need to roll up your sleeves and help in the areas where you see help is needed. Especially now, as we live in an era where some women want everything given to them, always remember, ladies: to whom much is given, much is required, so I do not want you to think this is just about you, having no responsibility. We all have roles to play in our success journey; however, for now, I want to encourage you, woman, that you are more than society has shown you to be. You are more, just more.

The Bible teaches us to show honor to the woman. Before I go any further, disclaimer alert: we understand that all women are not worthy of this treatment. In later chapters, I will talk about that just as all men are not worthy of respect; however, as a biblical man led by God, it is your duty to understand how we live our day-to-day lives while in this sinful world. (Disclaimer over.)

Now back to the pressing matter. Jesus is supposed to be our example. The Bible says, "be ye holy, as I am holy" (1 Peter 1:15–17). That word *holy* means to be set apart from the rest of the world. So he is our example that we should model ourselves after. I want to speak very briefly regarding what men need to ask of God.

Gentlemen, given our aggressive nature to hunt, we should always ask for a spirit of discernment (ability to judge well). You see, as men—as leaders—we are supposed to seek God's approval and not the acceptance of our little man. I am sure you know what I mean, but if not, you will get it later.

But before I start to ramble, let us get back to business. We as men must understand the importance and how precious you are, so we must always seek the Bible's response as to how we treat a woman; and Jesus is our greatest example as to how to treat a woman. Let us look at how Jesus Christ himself, according to Scripture, treated the woman. Jesus Christ has done more to elevate women's status to a position of high honor and respect than any man alive or dead. I bet you that statement surprises you, huh?

History is loaded with bad examples of how men have used their superior size and strength to intimidate, dominate, and at times, abuse women. As of this book's writing, I am currently in Iraq working on a contract, so I get an entire glance at how this side of the world still looks at a woman. However, I have also traveled and worked in Kuwait and Afghanistan, and in these cultures and religions today, they still treat a woman on a level beneath men. There are far too many cases of women being abused by men verbally, psychologically, and physically. History has not been kind to women, and on behalf of all men, I apologize.

When Jesus came along, he changed all that not in word but in his actions toward them. To God be the glory. So now I am just trying to show you there has been a change, although man has been resistant. Jesus demonstrated a high value on women by recognizing their intrinsic value as persons. For Christ, women have an intrinsic value equal to that of men. Jesus said, "…have you not read, that he which made them at the beginning [The Creator] 'made them male and female'" (Genesis 1:27; Matthew 19:4).

Women are created in the image of God just as men are. Like men, they have self-awareness, have personal freedoms, a measure of self-determination, and personal responsibility for their actions.

Jesus regularly addressed women directly while in public. It was very unusual for a man to do so during those times (John 4:27). The disciples were amazed to see Jesus talking with the Samaritan woman at the well of Sychar (John 4:7–26). He also spoke freely with the woman taken in adultery (John 8:10–11). Luke, who gives ample attention to women in his Gospel notes that Jesus spoke publicly with the widow of Nain (Luke 7:12–13), the woman with the bleeding disorder (Luke 8:48; Matthew 9:22; Mark 5:34), and a woman who called to Him from a crowd (Luke 11:27–28).

He showed a high value He placed on women by ministering to them vitally and practically, both physically and spiritually. Numerous healings and the casting out of demons from women display Jesus's care and concern for women.

Several such incidents are only briefly recorded. Jesus healed Peter's mother-in-law and allowed her in return to minister to Him (Mark 1:30–31; Matthew 8:14–15; Luke 4:38–39). Christ healed a woman who was bent over for eighteen years (Luke 13:10–17). Courageously, on the sabbath and inside the synagogue before hostile religious leaders, Jesus helped and defended this poor woman. He spoke to her, tenderly placed His hands on her, and caused her to stand erect, for which she glorified God. He then acknowledged her equal standing with men in Israel's religious heritage by referring to

13

her as a daughter of Abraham (John 8:33, 39). Ladies, you are not objects to be dismissed at will.

There were many other instances in which he was kind to women; it did not matter if they were sinners, poor, or sick, and he made sure they were better than when he left them. Please, let us not forget that after the death of Jesus, it was a woman that he first showed himself to. So even then, God held a woman in high regard. If we can help, it is my thought process that we shouldn't speak harshly to women—especially a Godly woman. Will the real men please stand up? Women are searching for you. Can you imagine the love that a man displays with his daughter if he tries to have that type of love, but more significant, to his woman? What a difference the world would be. Here is a question to all men: if God designed a woman for the man, what gives us the right to mistreat her? I will wait on that answer.

More importantly, ladies, why do you accept any old thing? Ladies, you must know your worth. You cannot continue to take anything from a man, mainly to have a man. An old song was out, some years back, in which the lyrics said, "Having a piece of man is better than having no man at all." I ask you, is that what are we doing now? Do you think so little of yourself that you take anything to have a man? I am taking a quote from the cartoon lion king: remember who you are. Or find out who you are. Do you not understand your power?

Wars are fought over a woman; men kill just to have the right to be with you. Men are in jail today over the simple right to be your man. Although I understand it is not easy being a woman, but you need to understand your power. Understand how precious you are. Just like Alicia Keys said it best, "A real man knows a real woman when he sees her, and a real man just cannot deny a woman's worth." I wholeheartedly believe that; however, the key is that you as woman must know it and believe it.

What is a woman worth? What is the value of a woman? If you are reading this now—and with all the examples I have given you regarding Scripture as to how important a woman is to this Earth by way of our lord and savior, Jesus Christ—yet you are not beginning to understand this, just stop reading and put this book down. You are not ready yet. If you are getting it with understanding, please keep reading but I go deeper backed by scripture. Let us talk about who you are ladies. Stop questioning yourself because someone does not get you. Their opinion says nothing about your worth, so go ahead and flip the page and let us continue to build you up woman. Sisters, rise to your high place.

CHAPTER 2

You Are Strength

Who can find a virtuous woman? For her price is far above rubies.
—Proverbs 31:10

You are worthy of love and affection, and you are never too much. You are always enough; you are precious; you are a diamond, a rose—the most stunning of all of God's creations. Why would I say this? It is because, for the right man, you are his everything. You are worth more than you can imagine, your worth surpasses all earthly things, and you are worth dying for. When you understand who you are, the spirit that you carry will know that you are in the plans of God, and you are going according to the purpose, intent, and will of the Father. You must understand his meaning in your life, for you are a woman of strength.

The Bible speaks about the Holy Spirit that proceeds from the Father. Jesus said I am not going to leave you alone, meaning the helper will be on the way—the strengthener. Hence our Father declared that you are the woman of strength, so you are here to strengthen. As a woman, you are the helper—the strengthener—and you possess the same character as the Holy Spirit; you need to understand who you are. You will never fail if you understand that you are a strengthener.

We know that there is no home without a woman, correct? Understand this with a revelation that when I speak of a home, I am not talking about a house. A woman is there to build. Yet she is regarded as a weaker vessel. They say that you are weak, but don't take that as something wrong because this is all a part of God's plan. Take Jesus for example. Jesus became poor so that we can be rich, so you are weaker so that they can be strong. You [women], the giver of strength, for you are the strengthener—that is who you were from the beginning because it was all in his purpose, plan, and will.

If you understand who you are, you will know that we need you even though you are regarded as a weaker vessel. So you are there to strengthen us when your family—husband and children—is out there. It is fine let them be recognized; the one who is behind everything is a woman. They see you in your children and husband. That is why the Holy Spirit is regarded as a person; although they say he to refer to the Holy Spirit, we know that there is no gender in the spirit. It is you; so, women, celebrate and embrace yourselves.

You know, I was studying the woman of a noble character—the woman of courage who is who you are for you possess such character. I fell in love with this character of this Shunammite woman, as it shows that she was bold; it reveals the strength that is in woman—the man of God was always passing by. The Bible says the woman said to her husband, "Let us build an upper room for the man of God, and let us invite him for a meal." It was the woman who initiated this, not the husband. Such boldness. If the husband were in the natural, he would have thought of something else, asking, "Why you are saying this man of God must come and stay here?" and "We ought to build an upper room for him" and, again, "You cook."

Because the Shunammite woman knew the plans and thoughts of God, for she was serving in the kingdom of God. When we speak of serving, even giving is part of serving, so she said to her husband, "Why do not we make an upper chamber for this man of God, so that whenever he passes, He will rest and continues with his journey" (2 Kings 4:10). That was a form of giving in the ministry. That woman had everything; she was rich. And when we speak about giving, it is not necessarily giving out money; when you serve the Father, you can give with anything as long as the Holy Spirit leads you. For so God loved the world that He gave with his only begotten son (John 3:16).

There, he did not give money, so this woman gave in this ministry of the man of God Elisha.

So women give, not expecting something to be given back to them; the Father searches for what you lack in your life. That is why we say, "Humble yourselves, and he is the one to lift you." You do not have to give for the Father to provide you with what you want in return, for he knows you, your beginning, and your ending.

The Shunammite woman gave with no expectations in return, but the Father searches your heart. Scripture says all these great promises are ours, so let us do away with everything that contaminates us. The rewards are ours, yet it is the Father who rewards us; for he knows where you are lacking. God knew her wants because of her heart, so she was rewarded with a child.

When will we understand the importance of a woman? Do we have to get knocked on our heads first? I do not have this answer, but I do know that the world would not be the same without women in our lives. I mean, without a woman, there would be no new life; even at the beginning of humanity, God put woman on Earth to accompany man. Many Bible verses about women show their strength time and time again during hardship, life's most fearful moments, and in happy times too. The Bible seems to love woman so much that wisdom was called her. Ladies, you are so special, but it does not mean anything if you as the woman are not able to grasp it.

> God is in the midst of her; she shall not be moved; God will help her when morning dawns. (Psalms 46:5)

> She is more precious than jewels, and nothing you desire can compare with her. (Proverbs 3:15)

Women are more valuable than some of the most precious items on earth, so we need to treat them well and care for them and they will return with love.

> Nevertheless, in the Lord woman is not independent of man nor man of woman; for as woman was made from man, so man is now born of woman. And all things are from God. 1 Corinthians 11–12

Men and women rely on each other. God made them equal partners in life, and they should respect each other always.

The importance of a woman. My God, I can go on for days. Whatever you give a woman, she will make greater. If you give her sperm, she will provide you with a baby. If you give her a house, she will provide you with a home. If you give her groceries, she will provide you with a meal. If you give her a smile, she will provide you with her heart. She multiplies and enlarges what is given to her. Although I am a big advocate of a good woman, we all know that just like how all men are not good men, just because you are a woman does not make you a good woman, and I will get to that in later chapters; however, for now, it is all about building you up, ladies. Helping you find out that you are more than society has led you to believe you are.

I continue to talk about knowing your worth because it has been centuries for a woman to be mistreated, misguided, and mislead, and I am here to try to change that today. We as men must learn how to treat you going forward. For this cause, I rely on the Bible so much as scripture says he will never leave us or forsake us, so he is always open to reteaching repeatedly.

God loves his daughters, and when he gives one of his daughters to a man, he desires that the man cares for her. In no place does Scripture teach or endorse that a woman is considered as second or inferior to men. So how on earth did this begin? I will tell you when man turned his back on God and decided to do things his way. God is clear in that he finds her so precious that he asks for special care to be given to them. A care that only biblical-based men can provide. Women are very capable of taking care of themselves; however, God did make men and women different, thus the physical nature.

We as men must learn, all over again, how to love you the way you need to be loved, and each woman is different. Each has its unique qualities. We must forget trying to figure you out—you are beyond our mind; you are a sweet mystery. We as men must allow you to be just that, and you will shine more brightly. We must understand the real essence of a woman, and it's beyond physical existence as a formless dance. Trust me, you do. When you open up and let us into your being, we must tread with care and tenderness. We do not need to understand you with our mind; we need to love you and feel your heart, not just your body. If we do this, we will find an infinite river of surprises and delights of endless wonders.

We appreciate your beauty—all of it. However, you are so much more. We must allow and embrace all your moods like the changing weather. We must enjoy the rainbow taste of flavor that you give us. Let's face it: we will never be able to "out give" you. Your heart is a sacred universe. Your body is a temple that we are blessed to worship. Ladies, here me now: your heart is vast like the ocean itself. We must meet you there, and she will show us the meaning of real love. She will show you the face of a goddess; you are a living smile. We cannot just listen to the words that she is saying because we may get confused, but we must feel her heart and listen to her heart's pure language. We must listen to the heartbeat of your soul. You are love, you are life, you are grace, and you are a mystery. The bottom line is, you need to be loved fully, fellas. Let us love her. That is all women want.

Yes, I know you may say some women are difficult to deal with, but this is why you take your time and get to know a person. That is your time, fellas, to decide: are you in, or are you out? We must choose to love the woman we have, and once that is determined, it makes no difference how you feel on any giving day. Loving your woman is a choice through all seasons. Never decide to love a woman based on how you feel that day. If you do, it will not last; understand that.

I tell people all the time not to follow your heart. I know this is what you are taught, so why would I say that? Here's why: the heart controls the desires, emotions, etc., and that could change from day to day; therefore, a decision to love her is based on a choice, and you must stand by that decision day in and day out, which makes no difference how we feel.

Men of God, where are you? It is time to stand up and show women we are also worth it. Let us treat our women the way God intended for us to treat them. We should study two things: the Bible and our women, because they are both hard to interpret. If you are a man and decide to marry a woman, understand the Bible says, "husbands, love your wives like you love your bodies." So, young men, if you are not dating to marry, stop wasting her time. But some might ask what should a man look for in a potential wife while he is dating? I came up with a few ideas on the next page in the hopes of getting one started, but I always seek God and his word for guidance on all things. Never, under any circumstances, should you pursue a man.

Call me crazy, but I do not believe that a woman should pursue guys. Does that sound like I have lost touch? Maybe, but it is against God's design. It is not God's way. Just as God wired women to get pursued, God wired men to pursue. You see, Scripture says, "He who finds a wife finds a good thing and obtains favor."

The man finds the woman, not the other way around. Now I know some will say there is nothing wrong with going after a man if you want him. I have heard that before; however, I have listened to this from only single women searching for that special one. I have also been asked, What if the guy I want is not willing to approach me? That is a good question if a man is not pursuing you. You must ask yourself, Does he want you? If you must question that, I say he is not for you. Ladies, if a man destined to be the head, he must first take the lead.

A note to all ages: women do not belong to us men. I do not care how many kids they have by us, or even if we put a ring on it; she does not belong to us. We like to say she does, but news flash, she belongs to herself. Now if a woman chooses to allow us to be in her life, we must remember she is a gift. And never forget that the Bible says, "Man who finds a wife finds a good thing and obtains favor from God," so they are a blessing. I believe favor is magnified by the way you treat her. Sisters, rise to your high place.

CHAPTER 3

What Men Consider Good Traits of a Good Woman.

Before we dive into this chapter, ladies must understand that these requirements will differ depending on the man you're dating, upbringing, and if he is a God-fearing man. Even the opinion of other women will vary, but I will go over a few things that I think that if you have these traits, it will make it extremely hard for a Godly man to allow you to walk away and let us face it. Any man that has good sense for that matter.

You must understand that no one is perfect, and just like men, women do not require perfection—just effort.

Love is an action word to me, and sometimes that action is self-improvement; and these traits can keep a man around long after he has explored you physically. So with that said, these are the traits of a good woman that I came up with to understand better what men are saying.

After speaking with several different guys from ages twenty-one up to sixty years of age, I collected their data and picked out what I think are the best qualities. With these traits, you as the woman may not agree with them all, but these are the views guys spoke of in what they look for in a good woman. They're not in any order. Please, ladies, I hope you're able to receive the opinion of the men.

1) A good woman is supportive. The best relationships involve two people who support one another. Just as your man is supposed to be your biggest motivator and inspiration, you are supposed to be his biggest cheerleader and coach. Now, that cheerleader should not take over and tell him what to do; men do not appreciate that. A better approach would be to ask, "Would you like to hear my opinion?"

Often there is something in us that when we decide on a course of action, the worst thing is for our lady to start telling us what we need to do. We do not like that. We know, at the end of the day, you are only trying to help; however, it is your approach that we often have an issue with. It is your tone. It is your delivery. You want us to speak to you a certain way, give the same respect and see if we listen more.

It has always amazed me at the every-man-for-himself attitude in relationships. You may not always get along or be in a good place, but relationships are about actively loving one another despite your differences. Some people covet their support even when they're not pleased by their partner, but that is counterintuitive. Sometimes, while we still love them, we may not always like our partner. Feeling supportive makes us feel loved, and remaining supportive during tough times can help save a relationship.

2) A good woman is self-governed. Now I am sure you are asking, What does he mean by this? Well, it is having control or rule over oneself specifically.

Nothing irritates me more than hearing a woman diminish a man's value and masculinity because of her skewed perception of power. I have listened to this way too much: "Girl, he was way too weak. I need a man who can control me or handle me." Ladies, listen carefully. Men do not want to handle you; we want you to handle yourself. You are not a circus animal; the lions at zoos need tamers and handlers. A grown woman, on the other hand, should only need understanding.

Good women are self-governed, speak appropriately, act appropriately, and are never adversarial to their men. They are good to good men because they have respect, not because their man must constantly put them in check. Again, a good woman checks themselves.

3) A good woman is balanced. Balance is one of the more undervalued qualities. You do not always notice it when it is present, but if you find yourself stressed out—seeing, talking with, or dealing with your partner—it's probably some balance lacking. Whether it's emotionally, logically, energetically, spiritually, or otherwise, balance keeps the peace, and a good woman understands that balance helps the man relate to them.

Having a balanced relationship does not mean you agree on everything; in fact, it can be just the opposite. "Be willing to disagree: a balanced relationship isn't conflict-free. Conflict can help to restore balance through getting bottled emotions out in the open, or it can act as a venue for sharing different perspectives." Not every relationship is going to be balanced in the same way. "Know what balance looks like in your relationship."

4) A good woman is introspective. Introspective is probably the rarest quality on this list (the ability to self-analyze). Most people can judge and measure others' conduct but seem to lack the vision required to see themselves honestly; they do not take responsibility or understand the impact of their actions. And that is because they do not want to be obligated to change anything that they discover.

Good women are aware of their flaws and seek to understand their weaknesses as much as their strengths. They can self-correct and admit their shortcomings. Taking responsibility in this way helps your partner see you more favorably and humanizes you during times when your relationship is on the rocks. It also causes men to want to meet you halfway by dealing honestly with their flaws. It can be kind of contagious. A guy might say, "Yes, I know you said you were wrong. However, I was wrong too." Introspective has that effect.

5)   A good woman is loyal. Duh! She is always on her man's side, especially in public. I learned this from a woman I dated back in Alaska—talk about a high-caliber type. When a situation came up, she never spoke about me to her family or Facebook or Instagram followers. Allow me to clarify: it is a difference talking about your relationship with people in your circle versus "down-talking" your partner in public because you're upset.

Being loyal means not lying or cheating or doing anything that you would have to lie. A good faithful woman is one of the most incredible things a man can have in his life. Still, it takes a real man to recognize it, which is why ladies should take their time and examine the man you are eyeing, as Scripture so delicately put it by saying, "A good woman is a crown to her husband."

6)   A good woman is affectionate. Now some men only like affection when it is attached to sex, but those men are just the exception, not the rule. In most healthy relationship's, men want to feel connected physically outside of intercourse as well. Touching, hugging, and kissing is something couples can get away from if they are not careful. Sometimes it takes a concentrated effort to nurture the physical closeness in a relationship, especially if you have been together for a long time.

Good women understand how vital their touch and their physical reception to their man is. It affects them, keeps their man feeling loved, and keeps the intimacy levels high. So if your relationship lacks intimacy, you may want to start trying to be more affectionate with your partner.

7)   A good woman is nurturing. Good women take care of their men in ways you cannot imagine. Ways that only a woman could. He can heal himself under her protection—when he is at war with the world, she is his peace; through sickness, she cares; through disappointments, she

is his encouragement; through self-doubt, she inspires; and when he is weary, she is his life support. I speak from experience, ladies: a good woman knows how to nurture a man. At least, my wife does, and I cannot tell you how valuable that is to me.

8) A good woman is capable. Meaning, she does not need everything done for her. Many women confuse being feminine for an obligation to be unskilled in certain areas that are considered more masculine. It could not be further from the truth. Men love a woman that can get things done. Men want a woman that enters the relationship with her abilities and strengths. People, in general, prefer to be around a person with a skillset, just like a good man has more than just some pipe to offer you. A good woman has additional skills that do not include her backside or her mouth. News flash, twerking isn't a skill set; I will let that marinate.

9) Intelligence. A good woman is intelligent. What I mean by that is socially, emotionally, and intellectually. A woman who knows how to act in public even when upset, can process her feelings, and have a good conversation. There is nothing like feeling stimulated by your partners' mind, and there is something so liberating about being able to trust your partner's decisions because they're wise and knowledgeable. A woman who does not need to be managed. And they also get more respect upfront from men once their mental strength is observed.

10) Finally, a good woman is secure. They know who they are, and they accept who they are. They do not seek constant acceptance or validation from people. They do not assume another woman is better. They are not bothered by the other beautiful women in the room. They have a majestic quality; in other words, they know their worth.

All the secure women I have ever known had this hypnotic power over men. And, ladies, I will not give you a man's opinion of a good woman without sharing my thoughts on a good man. You see, ladies, you are the key to greatness, but to stop going through all the turmoil that some men can put you through, you need to know what you want. I mean, how can a man—any man—begin to please you and treat you as God directs him if you do not even know what a good man looks like.

There is a saying that men have two heads, yet he chooses the wrong head to think within most cases. Well, ladies, you only have one head, and often you allow emotions or hormones to dictate to you what a good man looks like at that moment. It would be best if you choose wisely. One no-good man; can make a woman hate all men if you allow this happen? This is serious information you not only need to know but, more importantly, need to apply to your life. I want to share my thoughts on some traits on a good man. But please know I understand that he needs to be easy on the eye; I got it. One thing for sure is, if you find yourself being bitter toward men or even saying all men cheat or they're dogs, I beg you to try something different and see if that works.

You first need to heal from any pains or discomfort Mr. Wrong put you through and figure out what attracted you to that foolishness so you can make better choice in the future, if you do not, you will meet Mr. Foolishness again in a different body. If you are unsure of what traits a good man should have, flip to the next page, and maybe I can provide some insight. But you must be willing to receive the information and apply it to your life if want something different.

CHAPTER 4

Traits of a Good Man

A Good man obtains favor from the Lord.

—Proverbs 12:2

There are certain things a woman should be looking for in a man, and some men are clearly better suited for being loving partners than others. Yes, there are guys who simply are not cut out for the job, and you should not be trying to force it. Now this is not to say they never will be a good catch one day; after all, people develop over time, learning, and adapting characteristics over years and years of trial and error.

With scientists having spent decades trying to work out the key to why we fall in love, there are certain things you should look for in a potential partner which suggest you may have found a keeper. But you cannot leave God out of the equation when seeking or hoping to be found. Now God wants us to be happy and joyous in our relationships and find peace and understanding by way of Christ. God most definitely wants us to be happy.

Psalm 37:4 reads, "Take delight in the Lord, and he will give you the desires of your heart." With that said, if you are wondering whether to settle down with your current partner, or if you are not dating but will in the future, I have a few things that you should pay close attention to when dealing with a potential life partner. If they have the following qualities, ladies, never let him go.

Now understand this entire book operates on biblical principles, so without a doubt, your potential mate needs to be a man of God first and foremost. With that said, let us dive into these traits that I think you should look for in a potential mate. These traits are not necessarily in order, but if he is not about number one, kindly exit stage left.

1) He understands that he must be a provider. Scripture says, "But if any provide not for his own, and especially for those of his own house, he hath denied the faith and is worse than an infidel." This does not mean a woman should not work or cannot work to help support the home. But, fellas, understand, if you want a traditional wife, you must also be willing to be a traditional man, and he could provide for his family. You have heard the saying, and it's scriptural, "a man that does not work should not eat." Now there are exceptions to the rule; indeed, if he was disabled or something, that goes without saying, but a healthy man? Give me a break.

2) He respects you. While love is generally the number one thing women are looking for, it seems that many of them often forget that respect is equally important. A quality man respects you on every level. Your personality, values, religious beliefs, emotional needs, physical needs, general outlook regarding life, your flaws, and most importantly, your past; as you know, we all have a history.

   Never allow a man to call you out of your name, period. I see a lot of young women accept this treatment as being the norm. However, I hope even the young women wake up and acknowledge their God-given strength. As I believe, if you allow a man to call or say anything to you, it will not be long before he disrespects you in other areas. It would be best if you taught people how to treat you.

3) He protects you. Not that a woman cannot protect and defend herself, but he is there for you anyway. He will not let anyone hurt you. He is your knight in shining armor.

Now let me place a disclaimer: you cannot ask a man to protect you when you are flying off the handle; this goes back to a good woman knowing how to act. There are plenty of good men out there that will love to stand by your side, but if you are the one that is always causing the disturbance, they may not stick around long.

Remember, we are following Scripture here, not the streets.

A good woman is a crown of her husband,
but she who shames him is as rottenness in his
bones. (Proverbs 12:4)

I just wanted to put that out there. He will still protect you, but when you get home—if you make it home—you will have a lot of explaining to do.

4) He is confident/an alpha male. Confident guys are independent and self-sufficient. He does not need her to be happy because he is already happy with his life, and he is inviting her to share that happiness. Confident guys are aware of a woman's needs and how to fulfill them. Therefore, they lead her to her happiness!

True confidence is self-assurance. Confident men do not feel a need to try too hard. They are not out to prove anything to themselves or anyone else. They are secure in who they are, exuding an attitude of *I can handle this.* The more confidence you have, the better relationships you will have.

And just so you know, ladies, most confident men are successful men. Hello. Confident men are not consumed with their own insecurities. As a result, they can pursue women without inhibition. This puts women at ease, creating a sense of safety and security in the relationship. Establishing that type of dynamic allows women to let down their guard, open, and receive love.

5) He's kind, but not a pushover. Some overly aggressive men try to position themselves above everybody else. Some weak men avoid all commitment and confrontation. But a quality man manages to combine the strengths of both power and sympathy. He is kind at heart, yet brutal in battle. He does not start fights but finishes them. He is wise enough to pick and choose the best of both force and compassion.

6) He is supportive. Whether you want to be a rapper or a go-go dancer, to go back to school to get your degree, or to start a singing career, a good man will always support you and what you want out of your life even when he disagrees with it. He will never discourage you or make you feel like you cannot do what you set out to do. He is beside you every step of the way, cheering on your victories and comforting you during your defeats.

7) He works to gain your trust. A good man wants you to be comfortable and confident in your relationship. You can trust someone at the very cornerstone of this, and he knows that there is no foundation for love or respect without trust. He understands trust is not just handed over to someone easily. It must be earned, and then it must be kept. Trust, without question, is the most essential bricks when building the foundation of a strong relationship. Without trust, you cannot have a genuine love.

8) He always makes you feel beautiful. He understands that making you feel beautiful does not just mean saying the words to you; it means genuinely making you feel beautiful by the way he looks at you, touches you, and treats you. He notices details when you put effort into your appearance and reminds you how attractive he finds you, even when you do not think you are. A high-value man understands that whether you are in your sweatpants on the couch or in your evening gown heading to a gala, when you love someone for who they truly are, everything about them is beautiful. He holds your hand and lets everyone see how proud he is of you. When you are in doubt about your

appearance, he comforts you. You never want your man to lie to you, but sometimes he will lie to help lift your spirits.

9) He is not selfish. The basis of every healthy-and-committed relationship is the ability to compromise. If one of the partners is not ready to meet the other one halfway, the relationship is destined to fail. If a man can sometimes put your needs in front of his, that is a good indicator that he is a keeper. This guy is not narcissistic, and not everything must revolve around him. He understands that a relationship is not a one-way street and a partnership that requires constant compromise. He is ready to make some sacrifices for the sake of you and the relationship.

10) He's always improving himself. I tell my wife that I am working on myself all the time, whether it's learning new things, developing a new skill, reading a new book, or watching a documentary. A quality man prides himself on continuous self-improvement. He will always be intellectually challenging you and keep your attention. He is doing these things for himself, but the added benefit is the positive impact on your relationship.

Now I can go on and on regarding what a good man will look like, but, ladies, understand one thing: the ideal man that you have in your head may not exist. Learn to look past just the physical and see if you can see a person's heart. Take your time and get to know the guy.

As I am sure you know, some women want only money from a man. Yes, I said it. We call them gold diggers. I am bringing that up because those women are not looking for love, and they can look past the physical that the man may be lacking to get what they want from the man.

Why can't you, who seeks to be appropriately loved by a guy, look past some of the things that a guy may not possess physically to find someone willing to treat you like a queen? It is time to stop allowing the world to tell you what is attractive and what is not. Judge a man by his heart and how he makes you feel rather than what you think he can do for you. Once you have chosen your ideal man—yes, I say you chose him—it is ultimately up to you to decide if our so-called game is up to par.

CHAPTER 5

Equal Treatment

God created man in his own image, in the image of God
he created him; male and female he created them.
—Genesis 1:27

I will say this with all due respect to anyone who may disagree with me, and this may be the chapter no one wants to read. Especially some men who feel they are superior to women. You have, in today's world, different races fighting for equality. That is good. Well what about equality in your relationship? Either we will accept what the world's idea or viewpoint of a woman is—which sucks, by the way— or we will follow God and his Word.

Some prefer to follow the rules of the world, but may I say this to you? God instituted marriage, and I believe he understands how it should go. Often society interferes with how God has planned things, and we wonder why we struggle so much.

I have heard people say a phrase that I heard from one of my Indian brothers in Afghanistan. A term that says "a happy wife is a happy life." Now I know some of you women that are reading this currently will be all smiles, like, "That is right. You tell them." But I want you to consider and ask yourself a question. Did God, who created us spiritually at the same time and who gave us the exact instructions to multiply and rule this world together, ordain relationships to be one-sided? Just ponder that for a moment. If there is no me without you, then we are to be partners in everything. Our strength and weakness complement one another.

Remember, this is the same God that says, "Treat others the way you wish to be treated." The same God who said, "Husbands and wives submit one to another." Find in Scripture where it says that taking care of God's gift (woman) was supposed to be so one-sided. I mean, where in Scripture does it say the woman is the only one that should be happy? Riddle me that. That is for both the male and the female. There is a fifty percent divorce rate in the United States alone. Why? If you are not seeking God, that fifty percent is only going to get higher.

Scripture gives instructions on how to treat your spouse, and if you are not following that principle, you are already out of order. God must be the center of your marriage if it has any chance of working out. If you follow God, he will bring someone suitable for you just the way you are. But, ladies, know this: if you set the standard, we as men will follow.

We as men must be consistent with love, affection, and time spent, and you women must stand your ground. You must be that strong woman, and a strong man stands on God's word. So, ladies, that means you must know God's Word; you know what the man that approaches you is standing by, because if it is not God, then what is it?

Let me also say this before I move on: when I say a man should be standing for God, it does not mean this man is Jesus. He will not be a perfect man or Christian. It simply means he is more willing to stand by God's principle in how he treats you and understands his expectation of a man.

In the creation account of Genesis 1, God's first word about men and women is that they were equally created in God's image (verse 27). Neither received more of the image of God than the other. So the Bible begins with the equality of the sexes. As persons, as spiritual beings standing before God, men and women are equal.

However, here is the biggest issue that I believe that—back then and still—is an issue today. We tend to want things our way. You see, there are rules to the game, and everyone has an overseer. And with breaking the rules, there is almost always consequences to our actions.

Adam and Eve's disobedience to God's command resulted in inevitable consequences, but again, let us be honest if you will. I have heard people say that if Eve did not eat the apple or fruit, we would be okay; while there is some truth in that statement, let us be clear that sin enters the world not because of Eve, but by Adam (Romans 5). Therefore, sin entered the world through one man—Adam—so let us get off the Eve train. I am not saying she was not at fault, but we often forget if we are the man, take responsibility; and taking responsibility can seem like an attack if you are not ready.

Did not the Bible say, "To whom much is given, much is required"? Therefore, if we as men are deemed to be the head, then there are certain responsibilities that we must own. Consequently, it would have been up to Adam to say no at some point, right?

This is what I mean by standing on God's Word. Ladies, you say you like a strong man, right? Well there is not a stronger, more masculine man on Earth than a man who follows and stands firm to God's Word. So please, let us no longer say Eve was the issue alone. They both played a role in this foolishness we live in today.

Ladies, you always must search Scripture to get your strength back. You are designed to rule, just as men. Let us examine but a few instances in Scripture.

The Old Testament praises many women in leadership over men, including wives and mothers. It describes women in leadership with God's blessing with no hint that their gender should disqualify them. The prophetess Miriam is sent by God to lead Israel; she was Moses's older sister.

Deborah is one of the judges the Lord raised who saved Israel from the hands of their enemies—a prophetess and the highest leader in all Israel. She was a wife and mother and had authority to command Barak, Israel's military commander. They worked together with shared power; he as a military commander, and she as commander-in-chief.

Queen Esther had sufficient influence to bring about the destruction of the house of Haman, along with seventy-five thousand enemies of the Jews. She, along with Mordecai, wrote with full authority, "Esther's decree confirmed these regulations." The Bible praises the Queen of Sheba and the Queen of Chaldea.

Even priests consulted the prophet Huldah on finding the law's lost book and submitted to her spiritual leadership. Israel's leaders—including the king, the elders, the prophets, and the people—accepted her word as divinely revealed (2 Kings). The obedience of Israel's male leadership to God's Word spoken through a woman sparked what is probably the most remarkable revival in the history of Israel (2 Kings 22:14).

Not one Old Testament text says that God permitted women to hold such political or religious authority over men only because of special circumstances, nor do they describe these cases as exceptions to a scriptural principle. Although two female monarchs of Israel, Athaliah (2 Kings 11:1–3; 2 Chronicles 22:10–12) and Jezebel (1 Kings 18:4) were wicked, but so were most of Israel's kings. Scripture does not criticize them or any other woman leader of Israel because their having authority over men is an inappropriate role for a woman.

Instead, the Old Testament presents women in religious and political leadership as normal. So again, ladies, understand who you are and how God sees you. You are not just a housewife; you are strength, you are powerful, and you are God's child just as a man, so get up and stop allowing people to put you in a box.

You must read your Bible to get a complete understanding, because a man in our flesh will mislead you. Do not think of the Bible as a rule book; consider it a love letter. It is the story of God's heart to his people. Maybe that will allow you to feel more comfortable reading it. No one can make you feel inferior without your consent.

You, as much as anybody in the entire universe, deserve love and affection. Self-worth is so vital to your happiness if you don't feel good about yourself; it's hard to feel good about anything else. I want you to do better, to be better. Jesus says he came to give life and give it more abundantly, and that was not to men only. Learn who you are.

CHAPTER 6

Boys to Men

A man will always (and I cannot stress this enough) act right for the girl he wants.

The Bible is evident when you understand it in its proper context. When a male is born, he is a baby boy; however, he will develop into an adult upon growth. Ladies, this is nothing new; it is simply life. For a boy to grow into adulthood, it takes no effort. But, ladies, there is a difference between an adult male and a grown man. If you did not know, it is time you understood the difference.

I have already spoken to you regarding searching the Scripture for understanding. It will never fail you. So what does Scripture say about manhood? Scripture says, "In all thy getting, get an understanding." So you must understand what you are looking for, or what you're expecting of a man if that lines up with the way God designed a man to be.

Scripture said, "When I was a child [boy], I thought as a child [boy], but when I became a man, I put away childish things." When does a man put away childish things? The answer from you, woman, should be when he decides he is ready to love God's gift [woman]. It should be the time he is prepared to put away those things and take life more seriously. And that, my dear ladies, is what you need to monitor in your quest to accept a male in your life. You must stop trying to force a boy into manhood as you will continue to be disappointed and maybe poised to say men are not ___ (fill in the blank again please).

I am praying that as you all continue to read this book, your eyes will begin to open, and you will not settle for average going forward. When I speak, I speak as a man following Christ, so let us look deeper into what a man should look like.

The role of the husband, ladies, in the Bible starts with leadership but encompasses provision and protections. A husband will never influence his wife if he does not care for her. He can demand, and she may follow as a result. Still, he will never truly have her heart unless he provides for her needs, cares for her well-being, and protects her physically and spiritually; for the Scripture says, "if any provide not for his own, especially for those of his own home, He has denied the faith and is worse than an unbeliever" (1 Timothy 5:8). You must understand, ladies, how serious God is when instructing a male (husband) to ensure you are well-cared for.

> Husbands, love your wife and be not bitter
> against them. (Colossians 3:19)

It is okay to be upset with her, but do not stay that way, which is why it is so especially important to find the right one. We can no longer accept a mate strictly on the outer appearance. God says he judges the heart. So you must get to know your mate, and that takes time. Likewise, you husbands dwell with them (wives) according to knowledge, giving honor unto the wife.

Now, ladies, let us examine that word, *honor*. If you look that word up, it means "high respect or great esteem." Honor originates in our hearts and refers to the value we place on something or someone. Ladies, even the Bible holds you to a standard of great regards. This is what I have been saying throughout this entire book: know who you are.

God loves his daughters, and his commandment to a man was to love her; and when he gives his daughters to a male, he desires that the man delicately cares for her. In no place does Scripture teach or tell the woman to be second-rate or inferior to men. Instead, he finds them so precious that he asks for special care to be given to them.

Women are strong and very capable of taking care of themselves. God did make men and women different, and thus, due to the physical nature and strength of a man, she is to be managed with grace and gentleness. God did not create men to lord over any woman, nor did he create women to wait on men. He made us to work together as a team.

So today, right now, I want to send out a special tribute to all women everywhere who are the strength of life, the rock of her family, the gentle heartbeat to her children, the tears to her parents, the joy to her soulmate, the inspiration at her work, the support and love of her friends, the mystique in society, the leader of love and life, and the apple in Adam's eye. God introduced us to Eve, and although she was not perfect, you are a tribute to existence and stem from a woman's power.

When a good woman is found—I mean a good woman—and you do not rush to get in her pants and take the time to know her, it can be one of the most pleasant experiences you'll ever encounter. Let us talk about how a man is supposed to treat you—a biblical man.

CHAPTER 7

How a Man Loves You

Husbands, love your wife as Christ loved the church God.

—Ephesians 5:25

Ladies, the Scripture says it better than any man alive. If you are a woman married now or hope to be married in the future, you need to search the Scripture to determine how a man is supposed to treat his wife. Preferably, you search before becoming a wife. Why am I speaking about wife so much, you may ask? It is because you should not allow your time to be wasted. The goal, biblically speaking, should be becoming a wife; nowhere in Scripture talks about dating.

With this information, you must first understand how society has diluted Scripture. Scripture says, "Jesus is the same yesterday and today, and forever" (Hewbrews 13:8). Which means he has not changed, but we have. Our love for him has. We prefer to put the Bible down and go off our feelings. It is no wonder marriage has such a high divorce rate.

Nowhere in Scripture does it mention dating; that is a society thing. I want to bring you back to Scripture, and yes, you can still enjoy your life. So, ladies, the point is this: while we are following society and dating, if the goal is not for him to marry you, stop wasting your valuable time with someone who does not want to commit. You do not need that. Time is the one thing that you can never get back, and queens, your time is valuable.

The other reason I say we must return to Scripture is this very point. You cannot expect to get the things God says he has for you or even get special treatment if you are not following his Word. That is equivalent to losing weight and not eating correctly or exercising; it is no different. If you want your husband to treat you as the Word says he should, you need to be aware of Scripture yourself, which will also open your eyes to what type of man you need to have in your head.

If you know anything about Scripture, you will understand the Disciple Paul, one of the baddest disciples out there during his time. I mean, he was so bad that he could turn around a church with just a letter. Paul was bad. He made the statement about husbands, "love your wife as Christ loved the church," and gave himself for it. The love he had for the church took him to his grave. Now, ladies, that was a commandment. Were you aware of that?

Today the word *love* has been devalued so much that I have heard people say men should not marry for love. Can you believe that? We have some preachers out there teaching that nonsense. Talk about going against the grain. Ladies, understand that it's out of God's ordained order for a husband not to marry for love. Ladies, know your Word so you can discern what is true and what is false.

The word *love* is a critical concept because it is uniquely giving to man. Do you know that no Bible verse commands a woman to love her husband? None. There is only one reference to my knowledge, and that is when Scripture told the older woman to teach the younger woman to learn how to love; but no command. But you will see a man commanded to love, over and over, his wife.

Now, the wife is indeed commanded to do something, which is "to respect or revere her husband" (Ephesians 5:33). That is not a mistake; that is recognizing some unique attributes that belong to men and women that are different. A woman's greatest need is for love. A woman wants to be loved and feels love. God understood that, and man's greatest need is respect. However, a woman cannot truly respect her husband if he does not love her. God recognized that and has communicated that in his Word.

A man is supposed to pour all his content into his woman, which is why Scripture says, "Husbands love your wife as yourself," and anyone in their right mind would not want to hurt himself, correct? Let me say something about respect, ladies. I want to put the entire Scripture up for your viewing pleasure.

In Ephesians 5:33, Paul writes, "Let each one of you in particular so love his wife as himself, and let the wife see that she respects her husband." In addition to his command toward men, Paul says a wife should respect her husband. That is not up for debate at all. Respect your husband, period. That is the standard the Bible gives to women.

One thing I know is that men gravitate to the place where they receive honor and respect. If he can only get it from work, he will pour himself into his job. If he does not get respect from his wife but does receive it from another woman, where do you think the man will turn his attention?

I can provide, off the top of my head, one practical way women can honor their husband or boyfriend for that matter: allow us to fail sometimes. Why do I say this? Here is a truth that may shock some people, but men are imperfect. Now I know that is hard to believe, but seriously, we make mistakes.

A lot of women damage their marriage relationships by trying to prevent their husbands from making those mistakes. So you usually correct your husband, or tell him what to do. That is not the wife's role. A better approach is to allow him to learn through failure. Let him make a wrong turn. Let him mess up from time to time. Please do not allow him to wallow in self-destructive behavior, but let him be imperfect.

CHAPTER 8

A Word to Husbands

Husbands, likewise, dwell with *them* with understanding, giving
honor to the wife, as to the weaker vessel, and as *being* heirs
together of the grace of life, that your prayers may not be hindered.
—1 Peter 3:7

Men that desire to become a husband. Scripture says to "live with
your wives in an understanding way, as with a weaker vessel, since she
is a woman, and grant her honor as a fellow heir of the grace of life
so that our prayers may not go unanswered" (1 Peter 3:7). Notice it
said nothing about a woman's prayers being restricted.

If you are a male reading this passage, I challenge you to take a
step back and ponder on this for a moment. To love and care for a
woman is serious business, and it is not for the weak at heart. This is
taken from God's word; it is not something that had to be researched
or anyone's opinion. That passage is from the Word of God. I want
this to sink in for men on how important of value God places on a
woman. The Bible makes it noticeably clear that the responsibility of
leadership in marriage falls squarely on the husband's shoulders. This
is serious business.

The Scripture states that the husband is the head of the wife as
Christ is the church's head. A good husband loves his wife uncon-
ditionally and is a servant leader, just like Christ. Fellas, you cannot
search for a wife in the flesh, for our lives depends on it. Seriously,

guys. According to Scripture, God puts down the hammer on us men, so you better choose wisely. No one talks about this.

The modern world has created a lot of confusion regarding the wife's and husband's roles in a marriage. Most traditional gender roles are considered outdated, and it is no longer clear who does what. This confusion has compelled many Christian couples to want to know what the Bible says about marriage and the wife's and husband's roles in a biblical marriage. Thankfully, the scriptures are clear about this; all we must do is read and study.

The Husband's Role in a Christian Marriage

Leadership. The Bible makes it truly clear that the responsibility of leadership in marriage falls squarely on the husband's shoulders. Scripture says that "Christ is the head of every man, and the man is the head of a woman [wife], and God is the head of Christ" (1 Corinthians 11:3). As you can see from this statement, everyone has a headship over them.

That particular scripture has often been misinterpreted to mean that women are viewed as second-class citizens. I have touched on that in previous chapters; however, I cannot speak about this enough. We must understand God has the final say; he created all of us, and it's evident his way is the right way.

Unconditional love. In Ephesians 5:25, the Bible commands husbands to "love their wives just as Christ loved the church and gave himself up for her." A husband's love for his wife should not be based on her actions. He should respect, affirm, and always love her. Again, the word *love* is powerful, which is why Peter speaks it.

Peter tells us that "love covers a multitude of sins" (1 Peter 4:8). He echoes the proverb, "Hatred stirs up strife, but love covers all sins" (Proverbs 10:12). Some think that one person's love can blot out another person's sin. The only love that can cover sin in that sense is the love of Jesus Christ.

Sacrifice. Sacrificial action is an integral part of the husband's role as the head of the home. Again, Christ is a beautiful example of this. He demonstrated servant leadership by washing his disciple's feet. In marriage, being a servant leader means ensuring that the wife's material, emotional, and spiritual needs are met. How do we meet all those needs?

One of the greatest ways our wives or girlfriends feel connected with us is when they feel they are being heard and when they sense that they're hearing from the real us. For many men, communication in marriage consists of simply letting their wife talk while they drift in and out of the conversation with "uh-huhs" and "yeahs." You are not fooling her.

Communication is a two-way street. To cultivate true intimacy in your marriage, there must be mutual intimacy. Let me encourage you to be proactive in seizing these moments. Put down the cell phone and the remote. Grab a spot at the kitchen table or on the couch and connect. Do not worry if you feel like you do not have much to share; be fully present, ask follow-up questions, and dig deeper into her thoughts. She needs this, and whether you know it or not, we do too.

We must learn to date our wives again. One of the most potent ways to bring life to our marriage is to get out of the house together. It does not have to be expensive; hang out. Make it a goal to try and take your wife on at least two dates a month. Some months will be easier than others to make this happen, but this will never happen unless you make this a priority. Also, make it a point to take care of all the details if childcare or reservations are needed. It tells her, "This is important to me!"

If you want your prayers to be heard and not hindered, you must live with your wife in a certain way. There must be an effort to understand her and to know her needs. There must be a special solicitousness of her weaknesses and what she especially needs from you. There must be a recognition that she is a fellow heir of the grace of life and an accompanying bestowal of honor rather than belittling or demeaning. When we husbands live like this (with understanding, tender care, and honor), our prayers will not be hindered. If we do not live like this, our prayers will be hindered.

So concerned is God that Christian husbands live in an understanding and loving way with their wives that he interrupts his relationship with them when they are not doing so. No Christian husband should presume that any spiritual good will be accomplished by his life without an effective prayer ministry. And no husband may expect a practical prayer life unless he lives with his wife in an understanding way, bestowing honor on her.

To take the time to develop and maintain a good marriage is God's will—it is serving God; it is a spiritual activity pleasing in his sight. That is Peter's point too. There is a way to live that hinders our prayers and a way to live that helps our prayers.

CHAPTER 9

You Must Teach Others How to Treat You.

For this to happen, it all begins with self. It is all about how you believe and how you treat yourself, which sets the standard for others on how you demand to be treated. People learn how to treat you based on what you accept from them. Example, if I walked up to you and grabbed your butt, I should get slapped, correct? Is that any different with me walking up to you and saying, "Hello, female dog"? Hint, hint.

You are not going to accept that, are you? Then why do you allow any other treatment that is not up to your standard? First you must have a standard, and you must stick to that standard. It has been said in days of old, "If you don't stand for something, you will fall for anything." In other words, you cannot change what you tolerate. However, you cannot change people since your real power resides in yourself, but you can create different reactions in others if you change yourself.

Listen to what Scripture says: "Now to him who is able to do exceedingly, abundantly, above all that we ask or think, [hear me now] according to the power that works in us" (Ephesians 3:20–21). God has already equipped you with all the power you need to succeed. All you must do is stand on his words and stand tall.

Once again, you will never change the things that you tolerate—that is first and foremost. I am sure you have heard the saying, "That it is not what they call you. It is what you answer to." You can change things in your life if you stop settling. However, I must warn you: it is lonely at the top, and you must prepare yourself to be alone sometimes, to be talked about sometimes, or to be called names. Because with anything unfamiliar, there will be pushback, and when you decide to take your life back or stand up for what you know to be true about who you are, there will be opposition.

But guess what, woman of God? Scripture says, "God did not give you the spirit of fear." So you must get up, dust off your shame, and become the woman God designed you to be. You are what you choose to be *today*, not what you decided to be before. It is never too late to stand up for yourself.

Understand that you are love, you are power, you are strength. Now is your time to shine.

You must be more responsible for yourself and your self-worth. You must change the way you think of yourself; you must unlearn the things you have learned to become a better you, a more powerful you. Change your thinking about you. There is nothing more powerful than a changed mind. You can change your hair, your clothing, your address, your church, and dare I say even, your spouse, but if you do not change your mind, the same experience will perpetuate itself repeatedly, because everything outwardly changed but nothing inwardly.

You must have a changed mind. Teaching others how to treat you means that it all comes back to you. It is up to you to either allow or not allow specific treatment. It also means that you must first get a clear understanding of how you want to be treated. It means that you must take responsibility enough to write your own owner's manual. And you are accountable for living by your owner's manual. For some of you, it may be the very first time you ever even gave this any thought.

Remember, being accountable and responsible have nothing to do with blame. They are entirely different types of energy. Blame seeks to shame and belittle. Responsibility seeks to "un-victim" you.

If you are that person who may have self-esteem issues, no problem; speak to yourself daily. Tell yourself, "I do not allow people to yell at me. I do not allow verbal abuse." Please write it down and say it daily when you get up and before you go to bed.

The Bible says to have a vision. It speaks to write down your vision and make it plain (Habakkuk 2). Listen, you must first know what you want and what you do not want. Writing it down makes you focus and be clear about what you are going to teach others about you and what you tolerate.

Typically I do not recommend focusing on what you do not want. However, sometimes what you are not willing to deal with is a great starting point to clarity.

Depending on your situation, you will have some obvious beginning points. If you have been in abusive relationships, then start with, "I do not allow people to abuse me." If you are tired of people wasting your time by calling you up to relate the latest office drama, you might write, "I don't allow people to gossip in my presence." For some, these ideas will be no-brainers. But you might be surprised at how many of us allow these kinds of interactions to occur in our lives.

You also need to learn from your current situation. Ask yourself how you have allowed particular behavior from others in your life. Take one case where you are tempted to see yourself as a victim, or where you feel mistreated. Ask yourself how you allowed this to happen. You will be amazed at how often you may have ignored your own needs or desires.

Once you know what you want and understand or learn from your situation, you must own it and be proud of it. I mean, root for yourself like fans at a football field. Because everyone is not going to honor your requests or your clarity, and sometimes it will have to be you who treats you well.

You must be your biggest cheerleader because these are the facts. Some friends might not call you anymore. You must be willing to surrender those things that are not aligned with how you want to be treated. They necessarily must go away. And the test is to let them.

One of the things that keeps you hanging onto them is a belief in lack. An idea that there is not enough. There are not enough jobs, clients, gigs, men, women, whatever. And one of the best ways to find out that there *are* more than enough of these things is to be brave and selective, live by your values and standards, and watch what you do attract. You might be scared. But you will not be disappointed.

Ladies, throughout the tough times that you may go through finding yourself, you have to maintain consistency, and each day will get better—each day, you feel better because you are now the woman that God created you to be; you are woman—the glory of the man, the giver of life. We need you more than you can imagine.

The truth is, once you find yourself and take ownership of yourself, we as men will fall in line. Why? Because there is no me without you. If you all, ladies of the world, stand up for yourself—and not in a mean, malicious way but with your head held high with confidence—and be consistent, we will treat you better. We will love you better, and we will appreciate you more. You are now bone of my bones, and flesh of my flesh; you will be called woman, for out of man you were taken.

I believe the higher we elevate our woman, the less available she is for other men. When you break her down, you make her accessible to anyone she thinks will treat her better.

A relationship needs respect, and without it, we are lost. We are all different, and if someone cannot value your differences and respect your values and beliefs, they do not deserve a front-row seat in your life. Period. Stop hanging on to what needs to be let go.

CHAPTER 10

Understanding a Biblical Husband's Role

Ladies, just like how the spirit fights against the flesh, you also have to fight against your flesh; and there is a difference between a man loving you from the perspective of the world versus a biblical man's perspective—and you must understand the difference. It is challenging enough to live with someone as it is; now you choose someone who is not in agreement with God. My dear, you stay frustrated and be called "the angry woman." Scripture says, ladies, "In all thy getting, get an understanding." If you can see with an understanding, it will change your entire life. To understand is great wisdom.

Let us dive into this so you know the type of man you should allow to pursue. Scripture, by the way, tells a husband to love. And Scripture tells a woman to respect (Ephesians 5:33). Can we talk about this for a moment? We have discussed that nowhere in scripture does it speak about dating, right? However, since God created a man and woman to be attractive to one another before he considers being a husband, he needs to know how to love because that is a commandment. Besides, a woman can't truly honor her commandment to respect unless she is loved.

You see how the Bible tied those two together? When a man loves you, there is truly little that he will not do for you. And you can feel his love for you. A man is supposed to spoil his woman, and his woman should cater to him. That is love coming around full circle. I do not understand this selfish love that we see today. Selfishness is that attitude of being concerned with one's interests above the interests of others.

However, the Bible commands us to "do nothing from selfishness or empty conceit, but with humility of mind regard one another as more important than yourselves" (Philippians 2:3–4 NASB). It refers to an overly high opinion of oneself. A man serves and leads his family. *Serve* and *lead* may seem like a contradiction, but they are inseparable according to Scripture.

While the Apostle Paul tells us in Ephesians 5:23 that "the husband is the head of the wife," he quickly puts to rest any notions that this leadership allows for selfish male dominance. He completes the sentence with, "as Christ also is the head of the church." The passage goes on to say that "husbands should love their wives just as Christ also loved the church and gave Himself up for her" (verse 25). This paints a picture of leadership contrary to how the world views it.

A man is called to be a servant-leader—to take responsibility for his wife and children and to put their needs ahead of his own. He is called to demonstrate selfless, sacrificial love—the type of love we see in God toward his children.

> Likewise, you husbands, dwell with them
> according to knowledge. (1 Peter 3:7)

The word *them*—meaning wives, girlfriend, significant other, your crush, or whatever term that you would like to label a woman these days—the Bible says, "…deal with them according to knowledge." I do not wish to insult anyone's intelligence, but that word, *knowledge*—what does that mean? *Knowledge*. According to a Merriam-Webster's dictionary, that word *knowledge* means "facts, information, and skills acquired by a person through experience or education; the theoretical or practical understanding of a subject."

You see, the Bible speaks about studying the word for understanding, and I am saying to study also your woman because they are both complex and hard-to-understand. They are wired with all sort of sensors, feelings, and emotions, and most men are not built for those things; we generally just want to fix the issue.

We must study our woman; notice I did not say *women*. If you have a man or know of a man who has multiple women, I can show you an unsatisfied woman, because it is work. Scripture says, "In all thy getting, get an understanding." You cannot begin to love a woman, or let me say it this, make a woman know you love her without understanding that woman—and that takes time and effort. Dwell with her according to knowledge.

And, gentlemen, news flash: all women are not the same. What works for one may not work for another. The only thing that I have learned about a woman, which is universal, is a need to be loved, and that is a fact. What makes a man superman to his woman? It is the way he supports his woman. How he guides and protects his woman, how he is her biggest fan and will push her to her best self. The way he reassures her, the way he speaks life into her, the way he leads her, the way he communicates with her, or how about the way he prays and not preys over her. It is the way he *loves* her. This, my dudes, will be the way she takes care of you.

The one thing that most men are not aware of is this: nobody cooks for you, nobody cleans for you, nobody makes meals for you, nobody does your laundry, and nobody caters to you, period. A woman is always instantly looked at as someone who needs to take care of everyone else, and sometimes we need to take a day or two and do it all for her. If we are considered equal in God's eyes, we must do a better job of pouring life into our relationships as men!

Husbands, stand up for your wife, protect her from the attacks that come from the people close to you. Let your family and friends know that there is a line they cannot cross when it comes to your wife and marriage. If you must take sides, then always take your wife's side.

From the day you say, "I do," your wife assumes the privileged first-place spot of honor in your life.

When your spouse shares a struggle with you, remember that they probably need your encouragement and support much more than your advice. Start with a hug, not a lecture.

Husbands, if your wife is genuinely for you, she will be a reflection of how you treat her. It is your job to recognize your wife's strengths, her weaknesses, and encourage her. Often masculine energy will force you to believe you always know best, and in doing so, you strip away your wife's voice and natural gift. Treat her with respect, show her you are equipped to lead, protect her heart, and let her know your voices have equal weight.

Husbands, love and treat your wife in a way that she can be the woman she is fiercely and unapologetically. If you do not like the way she is acting, look at how you are treating her.

You become more self-aware of who you are, and it is that you learn the difference between someone disrespecting you versus you feeling disrespected. Emotional ears hear from a place of the offense. Sometimes it is not what they said; it is what you are triggered by. And unless you know your triggers, you will see everything as an attack, and that is not always the case, especially when dealing with men who don't understand you yet.

CONCLUSION

God has designed each of us in his unique way. He did not make any two people exactly alike. It was not God's design that we mistreat one another in any way. We must get back to looking at each other as teammates when it comes to love. Support each other, encourage each other, motivate each other, trust and communicate, apologize, and forgive one another if you genuinely want to win together.

We are meant to work together in everything. So neither he who plants nor he who waters is anything, but only God, who makes things grow.

> He who plants and he who waters are one in purpose, and each will be rewarded according to his labor. (1 Corinthians 3:8)

We are one in God; we have our journey to prosperity through Christ.

ABOUT THE AUTHOR

Freddie was born in Dawson, Georgia. Since his very early years, he has had a passion for God's Word. He has always had a desire to teach the Word, but like all young people, he had to find himself. In 2015, his path led him overseas, and he worked and lived in the Middle East. In 2016, he found the love of his life, and it was at that time he made a decision to rededicate his life to Christ. Not knowing then how he would touch so many different people abroad.

Freddie has a very supportive wife—Katrina—and daughter—Rayna—who are truly gifts from above. They have been there from the start, always encouraging him to step out of his comfort zone to be the man that God as created him to be.

Freddie is very active on social media, always focusing on positive quotes in the hopes that if he could just help one person when they are going through something, he has done something great. His hobbies include having an open dialogue about the Word of God, traveling, watching sports, and spending time with family.

Thank you for all the continued support of his purpose, passion, and journey in life.

All praises to the Most High.

Make sure you check out the author's first book, *You Are Designed to Be Successful.*